REFLECTIONS

D1417664

Also By This Author

Novel
2050

Poetry
Rivulets

Short Story
Early On

Play

Angel of Mercy

REFLECTIONS

A Poetic Collage

Dave Borland

ELDERBERRY PRESS
OAKLAND, OREGON

Copyright © 2009 Dave Borland

All rights reserved. No part of this publication, except for brief excerpts
for purpose of review, may be reproduced, stored in a retrieval system,
or transmitted in any form or by any means, electronic, mechanical,
photocopying, recording, or otherwise
without the prior written permission of the publisher.

Any resemblance of the characters to persons living or dead
is purely coincidental.

ELDERBERRY PRESS, INC.
1393 Old Homestead Drive, Second floor
Oakland, Oregon 97462—9506.
E MAIL: editor@elderberrypress. com
TEL/FAX: 541. 459. 6043
www. elderberrypress. com

Elderberry books are available from your favorite bookstore, amazon. com,
or from our 24 hour order line: 1. 800. 431. 1579

Library of Congress Control Number: 2008939344
Publisher's Catalog—in—Publication Data
Reflections / Dave Borland
ISBN-13: 978-1-934956-07-6
ISBN-10: 1-934956-07-4
1. Poetry.
I. Title

This book was written, printed and bound in the United States of America.

Contents

LATTE LADY

The girl, lively, lovely, young, endowed,
Is under surging pressure from the rush
Of those well endowed themselves,
Intellectually, monetarily leveled folks
Living their liberal, philistine reality.
Loving their good lives that free enterprise,
In all its demeaning, crafty, fruitful ways,
Provides them all with such bountiful joys.
This individualistically centered society
Rewards these collectively oriented folk
The ability to stand lemminglike in line for
The lovely, Latina to calmly, dutifully
Yes, individually, professionally, to please
The surging upscale masses seeking lattes
Weekend mornings in their upscale tiny town.
The latte lady works behind the busy counter,
As the ball-capped men in designer jeans,
Who've doffed their top brand designer duds,
Await, in slender, faded cowboy-looking jeans,
Reading dutifully the Financial Times,
While conversing on their tiny cell phones
To respective wives on their way to early
Fog-bound soccer matches of perpetuated
Five-year-olds trying to score their own goals.
The lithe latte girl remains blithely calm,

Breaking twenties, fifties, for the four-dollar
Charge for double-shot expresso brews,
That await the liberal-living, weekend folks.
Peasants at heart living the good life
By the interstate that leads to Valhalla
From their affluent upscale habitat.
The Latina smiles, as she makes, finishes,
Her hundredth foamy latte with whatever flavor
Is sought by the Times type rushees, who stand
Impatiently, awaiting their special turn
To put in their idealistic, usual order,
Hopefully remembered by the latte lady.
This morning moment will set their weekend
Off correctly when joltingly, a phone rings,
Amidst the steaming and foaming of the milk.
Five or more grab umbilical vital cells.
But it's the latte lady who grimaces, answers,
Never losing a whirring beat while talking,
Blending dutifully another coffee delight
As the front door opens again as more
Pleasure seekers pour in this Saturday morn,
Seeking their lattes from the Latina,
Who satisfies them all in so many equal ways.

LADY IN THE WINDOW

The lady sits next to a cafe window,
Obviously with quite a history
Written over her narrow made-up face.
Blushed, lipsticked, many times before.
Eyelashes lean down to pouting cheeks,
As she sits alone filing pointed nails,
On this high-brow street, in this high-brow
town.
Eye shadow darkens an already darkened face
Gaudy, yet with a hint of a once-lovely sight.
One can sense remnants of orgiastic screams
In her tread-worn face from forgotten times.
When someone, somewhere, gave perfect joy.
She has scars of happiness, but not this day
On this high-brow street, in this high-brow
town.
Moments of life's passion have passed her by.
She now, methodically, files her nails, alone,
Killing time, it seems, at a table by a window.
Someone has loved her, once at least, no doubt
As she sits alone this grey bound day
In this small café she's been to once before,
On this high-brow street, in this high-brow
town.

ROW VERSUS WADE

An empty rowboat at bay,
Floats gently on the tide.
A simple plastic vessel
Lying idly by the shore.
Letters faded on the hull
It's name, Row versus Wade.
It bobs gently up, then down.
Blue bottom, white fringe top.
On board one gray, ugly oar,
Astride, port to starboard bow.
The tiny boat is tightly tied
By a slimy, twisted knotty rope,
Anchored to the bayside floor.
An empty rowboat at bay
Floating gently, as the tide
Flows from the bay beyond.
Tied by classic sailing ships;
Tall, white masts, like swans
Spreading fanlike in the tide.
These beauties wait for masters
To sail far into the sea,
While Row versus Wade drifts
Patiently, wallowing, forgotten
By a master of long ago,
Anchored to the bayside floor.

SASSY LASSY

A seemingly stoic, sly woman,
In short-cropped darkened hair
Strolls on a lunchtime break,
In the sun-baked coastal town.
Her tanned face cracks a smirk
When she knows someone spots
Her long brown thrusting legs,
Touting her womanly mystique.
Bright, blue eyes, give no bond,
As she strolls smartly, smiling,
Dismissive of expected stares
From those she always mollifies.
In a scene from her favorite film
That plays in daily reruns
In her theater, of a gifted life
Few feel in their unnoticed roles.

THE TENNIS SET

The tawny tennis set,
Come their merry way,
From springtime games,
To their luncheon chat.
Husband's woes flow,
Through twitching toes.
They exchange mirth,
Sexual give and take.
Giggles, laughter reign,
Around the luncheon fare.
All tall, splendid legs,
In tennis-blended dress.
Beauty, fun, success,
Another, warm, spring day
Success, life is good
For the tawny tennis set.

WAITIN' FOR THE BUS

PROLOGUE

Waiting for the bus on a cold wooden bench.
Dark, pained faces from lives spent waiting.

DIALOGUE

"It's cold, man, blowing cold," the man said.
"That damn bus ain't never gonna come for us."
"That's life's fairness," his tan lady replied.
"We'll always be waitin', day and freezin' night.
"When's it going to be our time?" he asked her,
"When they won't be looking right through us,
Passing us by, eyes fearing us, pegging us?
When's that day comin' when we don't need no bus?"
"Soon, I hope, 'cause then we'll be driving past
This freezing, broken bench, you wait 'n see.
Someday, we'll be driving by, eyes 'n nose up,
Lookin' off past this ugly, busted, memory.
Can't wait 'til it's empty, I'm telling you."
"Here it comes, wait's over for another day."

EPILOGUE

The old, paint-faded bus stops; they climb aboard.
Folks who've waited so long, finally on their way.

FIELD OF BROKEN LIMBS

Once a full forest of upswept aging majesty,
Shambled now, dying, browning needled firs,
A posed depot of discarded Christmas trees.
This field cries from their tortured death.
An unfought battle, innocence slashed away,
Of majestic, forgotten, green-spired pines.

A MAN IN WOMEN'S CLOTHES

A man in women's clothes?
Not what you might think.
No transvestite here.
No, flimsy, fluttering pink.
Just a man waiting, coolly
Patiently for an icy beer.
Plopped in the only chair
Hidden, as his woman shops,
For the bargain of the year.
80% off the discounted tag
Nothing left, looks to him
But, a bargain's a bargain
To his woman who shops.
"Special fits, near perfect,"
The saleslady seriously says.
"Looks perfect on you, my dear."
The hungry hordes pull, seize,
Searching, sizing, squeezing,
As he humbly yawns his cares
Sinking deep into the chair,
As his woman, who apparently
Finds the nugget of the day,
A color he's never seen before.
A duck out of water he is.
No man should stop in a store
While his woman shops for more.

SNAPSHOT OF THE FIRST DAY OF SCHOOL

She stands, perfectly straight.
In the corner under the oak.
White dress, with a red belt.
Her colors blended as a fresh
Bouquet of just-picked flowers.
Mother peeks through the lens
Waiting for her to move a bit
Into a new break of morning sun.
Her dimpled set aside smile
Belies her underlying fears
Of leaving this safe haven
Where mother and father reign
To go to a place called school.
From a place she always been
To somewhere she's never seen.
She wants to go, she wants to stay.
As the camera clicks this time,
The picture from her first day
Returns from so very far away
In faded black and white,
Of that little girl, a mother now,
Well remembers her subtle tears
On another glorious morning's day
As now her daughter goes to school.
Will her fears fade to obscurity?
Flashed rites passed to another time.

LADY IN WAITING

The brown lady sits posed,
As a small-framed portrait
Contemplating on her stool.
She pauses, in reflection
On her midmorning break
On this, her first day back
After a restful Sunday off.
She sits, gray hair bunned.
A soft brown perfect face
Of dignity, eyes now closed.
By her side her backlog
Hangs on a rail, patiently,
Awaiting her sewing skills,
As she pauses for a moment
To pray quietly on her life
Of drawing pay for her work.
The Brown lady sits silently.
Her job, to turn duckling
Styles into swanlike fare.
Dresses once tight, now fit.
She thinks, prays, smiles,
Of her life, a heart filled
From thoughts of her children
Whose lives she's bettered
By her special sewing skills
Six ten-hour days each week.
Her head slowly looks upward

Revealing her gentle tan face,
Crinkled lines full of peace.
She shrugs, repumps the pedal,
A once portrait now becomes
A moving picture of perfection
Artfully mending human wear.

THE ODYSSEY OF THE BLUE MOON CAFÉ

The sanitized-smelling diner
Has four early morning souls
Who hover over their papers;
The Local Times, or of New York.
Coffee's slurped in unison.
Menus written on the wall
Ten chef specials every day,
But breakfasts are up now.
Bacon, hash browns, local grits.
Owner Theo is dark, a Greek.
Efficient, unsmiling, serious.
"When your order's up, I call,"
He politely says, adding "Sir."
Music of his Greek countryside
Soothes the gloomy morning pall
As it plays off the taverna wall.
In minutes, number 125 is up.
Theo smiles at the feta omelette.
A line grows of the usual souls
On their way to work, no doubt,
As the Greek country airs play on
Over the morning breakfast crowd.
Theo the Greek is living a dream.
He's in America and also his Greece.
With moussaka, baklava, dark coffee,
Blended with native-dancing sounds,
A wanderer who never left his home.

IF YOU TAKE TIME

Life flees by

Moments gone.
Memories flash.
Hope seeps on.
Thoughts, warm.
Pressures knead
Their woven web,
Entangling all.
Remember, tomorrow
Is another day
If you take time.
Yesterday's gone
Vanished by today.
Tomorrow's unknown.
Days fly on fast.
Some smiles, hopes.
Some fears, alone
Remember, tomorrow
Is another day,
If you take time.

MAN READING ON A BENCH

He sits, Lincoln looking,
Plopped on the iron gray bench
Perched on a green-veiled ridge
By the million-dollar marina
Meant for the absent, rich folks
Of a perfect day in Sarasota Bay.
His riches are tightly held between
Monstrous wrapped gnarled hands,
No doubt from prior toughened days.
His 401 plan seems to be his book,
As his Goodwill garb seems to say.
Slowly, he raises his head to look
At a solo traveler coming his way.
Crinkled smile is a perfect word
For his gentle acknowledgment today.
Slowly like a drawbridge he lowers
His craggy face to the book below,
Into his space of words, so loved.
Each man's treasure is relative.
A castle, a Lexus, a quiet walk.
Power of escape through miles,
Or those of painting, of scribing.
For this man, he loses this world,
When in his paragraphed paradise.
Thousands of years tightly squeezed
Through his forty-some-odd years.
He looks up again, now with tears,

From words that penetrate his mind,
His world is far beyond the marina
Of worldly wealth portrayed below.

ON THE FRINGE

The winners at the Emmy Shows,
That everyone seems to watch,
Celebrities fighting for limelight,
Are people I've never seen or known.
Not that I want to watch them.
Their humor, their persona, their antics,
Trouble my age of settled lyrics,
Remembered melodies, pure comedy.
It's all become noise over noise over.
I'm on the fringe of this society
An albatross of my own making, I guess.
Life today seems senseless, except
The thoughts within my private soul.
People want more and more, it seems.
"Give me, it's mine, everyone owes me."
Oh, but make a mistake, "I'll sue your ass."
It's an arbitrary, contradictory world,
We have in this country, as it spins
Obsessed with self buying and selling.
Careless, concerning rules or principles.
Stop signs disappear, unseen I guess.
Red lights become green, no stopping.
Me, as I weave in and out of life.
See a nation of taking, not forsaking.
Language used to matter quite a bit,
It's now a trivial pursuit of the old.
Ecstasy, not a dream, rules the young.
Media twerps expound on their zero

Tolerance for understanding of events.
Knowledgelessness is boundless as it
Moves the dumbness envelope to extremes.
Flash your newfound breasts to all.
Who cares! Fuck this, Fuck that!
As the language of the gutter reigns.
Pervades, instills, totally demeans
The speaker, the receiver, who cares?
It sells, I make, I buy the good life.
Everyone's talking, from cell to shining cell,
Not jails, but calls to no one, just calls.
People are numbed by booze, TV, and games.
Grab the polls, media, and the arts,
Snatch the children by their hearts.
Goad, debauch one's political foes
We can win the war of garbage mouths.
No one takes responsibility at all,
Better to blame, before found out.
Our leaders, whatever the media promotes,
Are a band of self-created extroverts.
Beautifully cosmetic people rule this world
Selling bullshit as their ware.
Selling smoke to cloud the air.
It's a small family of those that
Impact, control our cultural world
Whether in the movies, music, sports
Or in the media creating news.
A small elite molds the thinking
Of this tuned-out sensual life.
People care for knowing nothing
Concerning our social atmosphere
Better to divert it, than understand

Values, as they slowly disappear.
As this tiny core takes control,
Small rules broken first, large scale
Destruction inevitably will follow.
As the cultural elite inbreeds on.

It's sophisticated bullshit, hogwash.
Selling its glamour ware, everywhere.
Selling their social content, beware!
God is out, chaos in, they're never wrong.
Yet, in fact, they're always wrong, indeed.
What one senses in your gut is right.
Disregard their message, it's theirs!

A GLIMPSE TOO MUCH

Don't you smile at me, handsome one!
Don't give me that pearly shit.
Got enough problems on my mind
Than looking at trouble in you.
My baby's home with Mom, right now.
Boyfriend, I guess, somewhere else.
Keep on walking, you handsome dog.
Don't need you playing on my mind.
Don't you smile at me, handsome one!

AUTO CLUB

Sitting by the park on a wooden bench
At the corner with the changing light,
I watch car after car of the auto club.
Drivers bound tightly in rolling homes,
Cell phones on, radios on, minds off.
Hurrying to where, for what? I muse.
Maybe to work, to home, to wherever.
What's the crushing rush for them?
In this perfect springtime day in May.
Light changes promptly, yellow to red.
They stop in unison, a two-minute break.
In a jerk ahead, the other lane lurches
Moving on their own unknown mystery way,
Windows rolled tight, destination bound.
Everyone, going somewhere straight ahead.
My seat on the bench is a perfect spot
To watch the parade of the auto club.
To see every kind of vehicle known to man.
Jaguars, high-tired pickups, top downs.
So many look-a-like jumbo, bullying SUVs.
Even antiques with antique sweethearts.
Yellow cabbies in black-striped Chevies.
Big men, snuggled, stuffed in sport cars.
Little men in huge-fendered battleships.
A T-shirted tomboy with a phone at her ear.

Some drive right through the red light.
One old man stops, even though it's green.
Roaring, deep-throated silver pickups.
Vans, vans, and more canlike vans.
Then I see my once-empty bench is filled.
Time to move on, I too have a place to be.
One last look from the corner wooden bench.
The light changes, the auto club goes on.
I muse, where or why are we all going?

THE ONE-LEGGED MAN

A little guy in a blue windbreaker
Comes hobbling from the 7-11,
Clutching a coffee cup in one hand,
While handling a crutch on one leg.
Along the debris-strewn walkway,
He hops to a center wall support,
Turns his back, slides down slowly
To the gray cement, no coffee spilt.
He lays the crutch beside his spot.
Settles snugly in his sidewalk seat
Against the wall of the busy store
On the crowded beach-town street.
Eyes covered by black sunglasses,
Blue jacket, à la James Dean garb.
T-shirt tucked into a black belt,
That snugly fits faded blue jeans
That cover his folded stubbed leg.
The second leg points straight ahead
With a white sock in a black loafer.
He sits straight back, fit neatly
Under signs blazing 7-11 coffee deals,
As reflections of moving cars pass by.
Against this wall of his sidewalk seat,
On the busy, peopled beach-town street.
A cigarette's lit with a magic flip,
Then up he sits, elbow on the sill.
One leg tucked, as the loafer points

Like a sword across the trafficked way.
Carefree tourists pass, some look down
At this peculiar-looking, peg leg man.
They mutter amongst themselves.
Chirps, chortles, laughs, guffaws.
They hurry off from the little guy,
Who gazes off from his special seat
By the 7-11 on the beach side street.

THE PRESIDENT

The little boy, nestled
In his mother's arms
As the hubbub of the crowd
Awaits the President today.
Far away, the boy drifts
From the buzzing crowd,
As the President has come
To the tiny town today.
Purses, bodies scanned
By the security in force,
Who protect the man.
People squirm, wait
As his arrival time is due.
Suddenly, from the street
Comes the entourage.
Then a smiling man
Waving, wending
Through a cordoned crowd
To the temporary stage.
The shouting people
stir the sleeping boy,
In his mother's arms.
He rubs his eyes to look
At the smiling man who
Waves right at the boy,
Who yawns and coyly smiles.
A boy two, a man fifty-two.
Two-men, two-boys, today.

PLEASURE IN THE SAND

Submerged in sand,
A discarded butt
Glows as a rose,
A flower to a bum.
Plucked from a desert
To new usefulness,
By the street guy.
He deftly adds it
To a knuckled fist
Of resurrected butts
Sticking up perfectly
Like sacred scarecrows
In his gnarled hand.
A time of pleasure will
Once again come to the
Savvy street guy where
Joy comes occasionally
From canned treasure
On this ritzy street
In an upgrade town.

CLEANUP CREW

Empty bar, pool tables clear, yet
Music blares as if a crowd's there.
Two guys, the morning cleanup crew,
Swap stories of the night before.
Slopping mops on fake, faded tile
Slide over late night's many spills.
Smells of rusty beer, light or dark,
Taint the wind-blown new-day air.
Hard rock sounds turned on again,
Revive noises of the evening crowd.
Forward passes thrown and dropped,
All players gone, all promises off.
All that's here is the cleanup crew,
Who swap and slop the night before.

THE CRACKERMAN

There's no doubt he's a Crackerman.
Wife left him, long ago, when he was
A drinking, hard-living Crackerman.
Still a narrow cowboy burned in tan
Skin scorched from blinding days.
Bright, brilliant boring-in blue eyes,
That pinpoint, pierce to whom he talks.
Life's been hard, yet sometimes kind,
When fun filled his crackened face,
In another life in a long gone sun.
Now, he's in landscape, our Crackerman.
Each day, rich folk test this craggy man.
Asking of sun, soil, water, and such.
The Crackerman passes queries easily.
He knows his plants, trees, and shrubs.
Even tropical fauna from faraway lands.
He strides through rows of planted gifts,
Overhanging tall, hovering, bending limbs,
From God's abstractions of earthly lands.
Greens, reds, yellows, splotches of blue,
Like a painter's world in his world anew.
His customers know he's a fine plant man.
At day's end, he folds a huge roll of bills,
As another sun bakes the Crackerman's face.

DONE DEAL

Six men at a table for lunch.
Cell phones, laptops on hand.
Two are techno-wired talkers,
White, bossy, trendy Americans.
While four, sit silently aside.
One Indian, one from Spain.
And two stone-quiet black men.
Technos lean, converse alone
About a pending "monster" deal,
Which is the word of this day.
Their motto, they both proclaim,
Is we all work together, a team,
For the bottom line, ie: profits
For all, for families, et al.,
Overlooking actual realities.
Two technos talk their game
Four others bide their time.

THE SPLENDID CORP

I'm walking amongst the splendid corps
In the richest town in the world.
I've been abroad England, France,
But, never have I seen them so close.
Aloof, pampered, looking down below
At the rest of us milling hoi polloi.
They play a perfect, protective game.
I gaze on their gilded playgrounds
For their special, full-scripted life.
Hoping someday, justice will prevail.
That our Universal Energy will balance
All on an even playing field of Earth.
Yet the glitzy meanderers and their wealth
Are not at fault, can't be blamed, I'd say.
They're blessed by structure most never know.
They're blessed by what they never understand.
Those that are without such material means
Must gather all that's innate, instilled,
That creates their survivalistic ways.
Unlike these who discard what others seek.
The paradox of this or every human time,
Is how a semen speck creates unequal lives.
My stroll is done; I leave the gilded scene.
Behind me, redundant laughter of their lives.

CHRISTMAS ECLIPSE

The sun will be out on Christmas Day.
As it warms the crusted snows.
Our tree will be bell-hunged glory.
The presents wrapped with tidy bows.
Another Yuletide gathered scene.
Each year melting away the times,
Into solid, silver, red, and green.
Memorized songs of Christmas rhymes.
Fade to memory as the Blue Lionel stops.
The egg-nogged punchbowl squats vacant.
Eyelids flicker, droop, slowly close.
As a Christmas moon masks another year.

THE BRICK PATIO

The brick patio is off alone
Away from the crowded street.
Muted from the bustling din
Of the finely gendered mob.
Cushy chairs surround tables
Providing privacy to a few
Who seek some silent time
A bit away from social sounds.
Angled classic brick design,
Brown-to-reddened clay cells,
Bring muted clarity to a few
Who cherish this patio's power.

THE DAY AFTER THE NIGHT BEFORE

It's now noontime,
The place is empty.
All tables filled,
Mugs, bottles, butts.
Stale, used, discarded,
Tapped and burned.
Music off, booze done.
Waitresses waiting off
In the wings for more.
Last night, nonstop
Their bait and switch.
Now noonday, high sun
Then midnight, full moon
A trailer for the movie
"Day in a Life of A Bar."

DUTY OF MONOTONY

"Our clothes chute was a marvelous thing,"
She said reflecting on years gone by.

Monday was every day for everyone's dirty duds.
Everyone in the house just whooshed them down the pipe,
Several times a week she'd organize the pile
That built up during everyone's busy week.
Come Monday morning after breakfast made for all,
Down the basement steps after coffee she'd go,
To tackle the huge pile of whites and colors
That every week grew in a concert of uncaring depth.
Throughout the day the roller washer hummed away,
And soon enough the clotheslines smelled of fresh
Heated, soaped, and cleansed clothes hanging,
Draping, usually, over the sagging, tired lines.
No one could walk through the laundry room at all.
It was a maze of sheets, sweaters, socks, shirts,
From furnace to the irrepressible clothes chute,
Grinning its grated smile ready for another week.
After another Tuesday morning of breakfasted kids,
Plus stalwart husband stalking off to the streetcar,
She'd grab her portable Motorola and head down,
To face her designated Tuesday chore of ironing all day.
She'd pause to smoke and push that iron over the board,
Breaking only for lunch and her daily Stella Dallas.
Later doors reopened, kids back from school.

It was a lighter day on Wednesday, only cleaning to do.
She'd start in the bedrooms and work her way downstairs, so
That by dinnertime she had finished the dining room in time
For her soaps to get ready for the dinner that night.
Thursday was always shopping day at the local A & P.
Her list had been made all week and it was followed to a T.
Very seldom did she stray from her needed foods and supplies,
Making sure that everyone got what they asked and she needed.
It was fun to get out and sometimes she took a drive,
Always by three she'd be back when the youngest reappeared.
Fridays she sewed and did things that she knew she had to do.
Then she'd get ready for weekend activities that she planned.
When everyone got home, all was in order and prepared.
We all knew what was needed would be where it should be.
Weekends were full including fun for all the kids.
Her husband worked at home on projects he liked to do.
It was a structured life, not varied much at all.
She did this pattern without complaint to any kids or husband.
This went on for years on end until everyone went their way.
The husband of forty years died and left her totally alone.
For the first time in years, she'd nothing now to do for anyone.
Everyone thought she must be lonely with no one to bother for.
Truth was she was happier then to plan, control her life
Than all those married years when she couldn't be herself.
Her monotony was a dedicated life others never knew,
She died, peace gaining over the gnawing of those years.

ODE TO WHITE-OUT

Oh, if only in this blightened, frightened current world,
We could be given some day, say on a pending frozen May,
A pocket-sized, everlasting quick-dry obliterating clay,
Of thick White-out to saturate our cyclonic-cycled swirl.
As quickened quelling moments erupt, penetrate, control,
The tiny-bottled ooziness, full of sloppy deadening hope,
Would wipe away penetrating pain like a proliferated soap.
As we live rationalizing days, dreams realistically find
Words burnt in a wooded plaque on an ancient wooden beam:
"THINK OF YOUR LIFE, THINK OF YOUR WORLD,
THINK IN FEAR."
A nightmare theme for the young and those yet to be made,
Who face terror-filled thoughts of a terror-filled world.
Oh, if only there was White-out to blot out their fears.

78

Where are those melodic forces now?
Who played that music of long ago?
Fingers pulling the bow to bare,
Frantic Bartok's country-dancing style.
Reheard phonetically by absent souls.
Those quiet, tombed spirits dwell,
In mysterious channeled needled waves.
Spanning spinning years, till now.
Soothing those who listened then,
As their world spun chaotically by.
Captured poetic sounds of metered life,
Flowing anew from far beyond this time.

PERFECTION BY THE BAY

One brown and white Chevy camper,
Alone in the large parking lot
Facing east toward Tampa town as
Day rises in brilliant warmth.
By the brown and white rolling home
Sits the king of his mobile world.
Absorbing, in shorts, the perfect sun,
Whose ray's strike his proud domain.
Talking to himself, happy, engrossed
In his silent, tranquil roving stop.
We all should find such a perfect spot
Where troubles fade, peace pervades.
When quiet quells life's fears.
A solo man living beyond societal swirl,
Leans over, turns on a Sinatra song
That completes his secret search today.

WORK WEEK'S OVER

Small guy, in tight Levi's,
Cruises cross the lot.
Work over, it's party time.
Huge sunglasses hide him
From anyone from his work.
Black, sleeveless T-shirt,
Spawn-muscled, tanned arms
Flaunting rebel tattoos.
He grips a case of cold Bud
Tight, in his hanging hand,
As he struts cockily to his
Black pickup that awaits
The guy's solo Friday night.
It's his time to be himself,
When no one watches too close
Or cares what he might do.
He can be totally himself.
Weekend's on, shackles off.
Got cash, Bud, his pickup too,
His weekend time to live.
The black cab door flies open,
The Bud safely on the floor,
Minus one popped can of suds,
As his weekend starts to roar.

SISTERS ACROSS THE STREET

Two sisters lived alone the last few years
In the old corner Florida house across the street.
Stella never married, a solo self throughout her years.
Sister, Mrs. Squires, older, prettier, married once,
Who's been widowed the past twenty-odd years.
In their later years, the sisters came together again,
To face their remaining life and pending death.
Stella, eighty-six with always a crinkled smile
Walked slowly on arthritic-rubbered legs.
Mrs. Squires, a straight-up narrow fireball,
Smiling, silver, stoic, living each day on and on.
Their corner white old Florida house, they kept
Immaculate, manicured throughout the year.
Their time spent with a circle of church friends.
There was no family left for them to dry lost tears.
Two lovely though not lonesome ladies of yesteryear,
Wending their way to eternity, each Florida day.
Then late last fall when the weather was very hot,
Mrs. Squires was inspecting the well-groomed lawn,
Brisk in her usual humor and lasting smile,
Yet, one could tell, saddened by sister Stella's
Broken, crumbling fall on their darkened driveway.
Uniformed attendants came in the pitch-black night
Buzzed around, then lifted and rolled her to the van.
First to the ER, then to a beachside nursing home,
Where it was said she would now always be.
Over the cooler, drying winter, less and less
Was one to see of candid, sparkling Mrs. Squires.

She seldom walked around the now-shaggy corner lot.
One day a meandering gray-lined cat crawled slowly
Over the once-perfect, manicured Florida yard.
Then slowly the front door creaked then pushed open.
Mrs. Squires gaunt, chased the intruder off.
Another month went by without her being seen
Around the weed-grown, grass-browned corner yard.
Until, yesterday when a police car slowly stopped by.
Then came a fire truck, followed by an ambulance
That overwhelmed the dried-up, weed-filled lawn.
Minutes passed, finally Mrs. Squires was rolled out
In a gurney with the familiar IV apparatus attached.
In a minute, the once-fiery, cosmic lady was gone.
The overrun, weed-filled yard, empty now except for
Bending tire marks that creased the unkempt lawn,
While curious searching squirrels slid down an oak.
The old Florida house of eighty years sits empty now.
Decrepit looking, straggly, overgrown with no memories
Even of fun-filled ice tea days under the lively
Live oaks, white-bloomed magnolias, on a crew cut lawn.
The sisters are together again in this life, waiting
On the beach for their home in their eternal corner lot.

EMPTY FACES

The look is blank,
Faces empty of life.
Scurrying clueless
In their artic land.
Thoughts distilled,
As quickly chilled,
Before fruition
Could salvage any
Human comprehension.
Bodies gluttonized
By everything, yet
By absolutely nothing.
Empty cares belched
Soothing selfish pain.
Wallowing to a drain.
Gum pulled off heels
Screeching of wheels,
People zombie away
Lives seen yesterday.

PENSIVE WRITINGS

The pot sequesters poopers daily.
Squatter's rights, you know.
Sitting, underwear askew.
Pecker resting comfortably
As gravity takes hold.
A time to think, to pause.
Natures takes its course
Through the tunneled tube,
Mind slows as the body
Flows refuge of the day.
The dark brick walls surrounds,
The pooper, who sits silently
On the horseshoe curve.
Plop goes his entrailed
Cargo tumbling to the pool,
Deep down, echoing below.
A glance to the old brick,
Beside the squatter's stall,
Scrolled names, slogans
Scratched on the faded wall,
Secretly written years ago
By fellow quiet crappers.
This pooper returns to business
As a perfect bull's-eye landing
Is recorded in the pool.

The squatter deftly unrolls
Paper as he pensively reads
Off the flaking, faded walls
Lines of prickly prior poets
Who, over the many years,
Pondered while they pooped.
Nasty words, nasty thoughts,
Promises, impossible to keep.
Scrawled in age-old letters
In this poopers' rendezvous.

THE ALLEGRO

A coffee bar
In deepening dusk.
Men gather, talking
In native tongues.
Unknown words to the
Silent looker on,
At the Allegro Café.
A nightly forum
Gathered on benches
Each closing of a day.
Do these foreign men
Talk of native cares?
No, just sharing life
At the Allegro Café.
Apart, three young men,
Americans, no doubt,
Laugh loudly, lying of
Women, past and future
Now fill present plans.
Another evening ritual,
At the Allegro Café.
Words, thoughts exchanged
Some from far away, while
Others, young, native born.
Sing beauty of human traits.
To gather, to talk of lives
In a warm, carefree night,
At the Allegro Café.

YOUNG MAN AND HIS BOOK

He steps slowly out of the bookstore
Into a shining day,
Clutching his private treasures
Of secrets, in a way.
The bookstore's in a corner
Off the red-brick patio.
A sign faded by the constant sun,
Reads simply, "BOOKS."
The young man stops, looks about,
Shields his eyes.
He shrugs, grasps his current find
On his Saturday reprieve,
From his weekly, working life
Between his weekend days.
He seeks old books, this solitary lad,
As from a time of long ago.
Dressed well in creased khaki pants
And shirt of something blue.
White socks snugged up his calves
A single man of pride.
He stands silently, musing in his mind,
Of a distant family.
Women have come and usually gone,
Only his books stay on.
Then, checking his watch, off he goes,
A newfound book, another day again.

IT'S COME TO THIS

Down 95 to exit 79.
Turn down a four-lane road,
Off at the second left.
Drive on to the Texaco.
Take another left a bit,
Turn into Sunshine Care.
"She's in eight twelve, my dear.
Go round to the back,
Be sure to watch out
For the numbers, my dear."
Number 812 is at the end.
Sits squarely in the sun,
Where it's supposed to be,
Smack between 810 and 814.
Under a fake-tiled roof
With a tiny green awning,
One of the colorful add-ons
For the folks of Sunshine Care.
A screen door gets you in,
Guarded by a pesky mutt
Of the lady's last abode.
She lived a life in Tennessee.
Raised five kids, don't you know.
Wallace, dear old Wallace,
Died years ago, in the hillside
Home of her total married life.
Two of her own are also gone.
She, alone, lives on, you see

In jam-packed Sunshine Care.
Meals, of sort, are made for her,
As part of the Ultra-package deal.
Aspirin, wheelchairs on the rocks.
Not much one has to do each day,
Besides get up or later go to bed.
A living center is what it's called.
For those, like her, too old to live
Amongst the usual world at large.
Little bowwow snaps, backs away
As this quiet friend who's come
To spend some time with the lady
Living life in 812 of Sunshine Care,
Who's really at the end, you see.

MEMOIRS OF A LADY

Had love from many souls
Over all my ninety years.
Put away, just a year or so,
My man since 'thirty-three.
Sixty-seven years with him
I miss his constant strength
Those arms, now in eternity.
But, got security and my God, you see.
Wrote it all down last year,
Right after he went his way.
Memories jumped alive, anew
Landing on paper of powder blue
I'll tell you, it's a tale all true.
So lovely, too, stories, oh my!
Things I did, fun I had, oh well,
But, got security and my God, you see.
Pass the sugar, please, my dear.
Coffee, two cups won't hurt,
Nor my nip of beer a day, okay?
Read The Good Book, never too late
To learn to live, to open the door
To see the Man, maybe mine, too.
Quite a thing what we call life,
But, got my security and my God,
you see.

TRIAGE

Beep, bop, boop.
Off to lunch they march.
The big balding boss
Beside the trendy blonde,
Then the short, plump guy.
A business trio in life,
Triangulared lunch confirms,
That the big guy's boss,
The lady is next in line.
The add-on pudge completes
The corporate trio roles.

ACROSS THE FENCE

The women stand across the unruly hedge.
Under protective limbs of ancient oaks.
In shorts, with little ones grabbing legs,
As raindrops ricochet off hanging leaves.
They gab away until laughter rocks the air,
Neighborhood telltales flowing to and fro.
A time of mutual friendship, shared concerns
That flow openly over their phonic fence.
A child's cry curtails their week-day break.
The women smile, wave, turn away, duty calls.

ANNUAL TREK

A calming, refreshing, early winter day.
Frozen frigid sameness pending continually.
Sporadic, reddened blooms peak out in full.
Drenched by autumns clear cold tumbling rain.
Flashes crack the sky in freezing windy airs,
As limping leaves lose their dried up sway.
Drifting ducks are deepening dampened down,
Shifting frozen drafts roll in from far away.
A distant November sun comes up anew, on cue,
As a single soul treks down now winters path.

A WALK IN ALMOST SPRING

I

A walk in almost Spring.
Can take you far and yet so near.
To your life, as it was.
To your life, as it seems.
This day of chilling warmth
Causes spilling heat to cool.
As you walk over steps,
That you walked long ago.
Up the same, now weary hill.
Past the school of empty dreams.
Strides then, steps now, as life
Graduates into your inner self.

A WALK IN ALMOST SPRING

II

As you pass, in half-turned glance,
A flag flies free, but just halfway
To note the swath of cycle cold
Of one young god gone in gold.
A few gathered, muted, crying loud,
Pleading for mystic ways to explain
In some simple way life's reality
Of those that die much too soon.
That school, that place, of emergent youth.
Propelling still-soft minds and bodies too.
Far into the sphere of earthly space.
Where so many, as I, still orbitate.

A WALK IN ALMOST SPRING

III

But on this rallying walk of mine,
Pushed by need for simple solitude
Past rows of slowly fading brick,
Fronted by flaking painted doors,
Causes me to wonder where I've been.
This walk, today, through cooled-down air,
Past multi-lived in places there.
Three decades gone, my god, what now?
The place seems similar, yet unfamiliar too.
Bricks, windows, huge, gray front steps.
A bit unkempt though, shattered bottles
Against the cracking, aged blackened curb.

A WALK IN ALMOST SPRING

IV

Sad portrayal of a changed, crumbling world.
The message slowly begins to grasp me now.
Walking over steps taken many years before,
Is that I'm lost in a noisy, frantic, world.
Not a bottle thrown away, but a dislocated soul.
Cars roar and screech in a sonic joustabout
Whoever, me, this day, happens in their way.
A mere person has no chance this day and age,
To want only time to think in pensive peace.
Give me a chance to walk in foaming water,
In breaking waves that roar in quickened quiet,
Competing with sweeping soaring squawking gulls.

A WALK IN ALMOST SPRING

V

As I return to the lifescene of my youth, I know.
I'm tired of all intrusions of peopled life.
When noise competes with noise, and noise again
Competes with discarded droppings on the street.
May solitude come to the volume of this world.
When there won't be ugly, piercing vibrations
From the clamoring swarm, piercing sensationally
Into my cotton-questing individual placid needs.
Somewhere I've seen bent orchids of purples, yellows
Curling round climbing stems, green to cuppened end.
Such beauty offered men who carry on a quest,
As I this day from the crushing stampede all around.

A WALK IN ALMOST SPRING

VI

So much has passed through my searching soul
Since first I walked this budding, learned way
Those that bore me have gone their silent road
Those I have born are on their lifelong trail
So, this day, on this familiar way, I softly hear,
Flitting sparrows hopping on newly moistened ground.
Dancing to a polka played on tiny ancient stones.
Searching daintily on fresh-drenched newborn green.
I muse, as I near the end of this searching stroll,
I feel so cleansed as the dropping warm, sweet rain
Falls on my upturned face in sweetened gratitude.
A day to blend that mellow past with my consecrated life.

BACK TO THE POND

The large toad wallows away from another day,
Pushing fifty and two fifty.
He ambles softly through his unrelenting life,
Belly full and overlapping.
The once-tanned leather belt holding hopelessly,
his third best suit.
A rounded shape, sloping down slovenly,
From a once-slender form.
Now, all of those slimmed-down dancing days,
Have long departed him.
He'll rise slowly, be off for another day,
Pushing fifty and two fifty
Looking to the narrow mirror of time,
Seeing a lean and slender man.

AN EDIFICE OF BLUE LIGHT

It's just...here!
An edifice of God.
Within walls of stone
Unseen powers of hope
For anyone, anytime.
Massive arches of love
Rise stoically above
Flanked by colored hue
Of joy, blissful blue.
Overwhelming peace
Pervades perfect silence
Of this place of God.
By any other name it's
Simply a silent power.
Edifice of myriad glass
Reflecting sunlit joy
Quietly, flaring out
From billions of years
Of light from far away.
Through prisms of peace
A classic beauty of power
Resplendent, resilient
From our Universal essence
Of love, joy, and reason.
This massive calm citadel
Harbors everyone quietly.
It's just...here!

THE OLD REX

Tattered a bit, still proud.
Red and yellow faded colors
Barely brighten dingy walls.
The Old Rex sits squatting
Snuggly between two remnants
Of a bustling, vibrant past.
The neighbors are now occupied.
Jewelry, gifts, still sell, but
The old warhorse lies dormant.
Tickets to a movie downtown
Just aren't enough these days
To fill seats of the fallen Rex.
The box office squats lonely
In the foyer, where Mr. Jones,
White shirt, red bow tie, jacket,
Sold tickets for every show.
He's gone now, dust to dust,
Like all customers of that day
Who necked once in the balcony.
Drive slowly by at any time,
Look at the Old Rex in decline.
In faded shades of gold and red
Once projecting joys of life
Now a beauty rests in sad decay.
Bring back the Old Rex, some say.
To the perfect glory of its day.
Hand-clenched couples of every age,
Clutching yellow popcorn packages.

Awake the flickering framed ghosts
Of movies and audiences of the past.
Turn on the multi-rainbowed lights.
Put up the black letters of the show
Of what is on and who are the stars.
The Old Rex patiently, proudly waits
For that switch to be turned on.
Who knows? Mr. Jones might return
To sell us tickets once again.

DEATH OF A FRIEND

A friend is finally gone.
Well not gone, really.
He's on a late night drive,
In his classic Beamer.
Top down, in cruise control
To new places up ahead.
Sick, yes, when he left,
Ready to go, no fuckin' way,
Never a topic for discussion.
Over recent days, months,
The will of a gentle giant.
A giant he was, not in size,
But of smiles, jest; his eyes,
That glittered, sang a tune.
Guts of a wounded tiger;
Grasping, fighting, swearing
At the goddamn unseen terror
That sucked his very core,
But feared his heart and soul.
Finally, gracefully, lovingly,
God called a truce, gave peace.
The Beamer was waved on,
To the gates of pain-free joy.
An eternal sigh was breathed,
A friend with a smile, a wave,
Drove through his final toll,
With only one hand on the wheel.

THE PARTY'S OVER

I'll be dead, deceased, gone!
The party will proceed, go on.
Someone may mention my name,
A memory of me may ascend,
To some of the Friday group.
Then, the two-man band blasts.
The usual white-haired guys
With oldies, no one knows.
Dancing creaks the oaken floor.
See, that mist above, that's me.
Overseeing life, as it churns
On its merry, unstoppable way.
With no thought of me, now gone.
So, I sigh, shrug, smile, then
Drift into the ethereal night,
Like mist on a car's heated glass.
Farewell, salud, ciao, last call,
I say voiceless, to mates below.

Printed in the United States
207864BV00001B/184-234/P

9 781934 956076